Cumbrian Communities and their Railways No. 2

Ravenglass:
Roman Port to Railway Junction

The story of the ancient port
and the railways which linked at Ravenglass

Peter van Zeller

**Cumbrian
Railways
Association**

Contents

This book is dedicated to the memory of Pam Conroy,
who saw the village into its third millennium.

Acknowledgments

The author writes looking out over the Roman harbour, from a house built by an engineer of La'al Ratty on the last remaining strip of the old Town Fields of Ravenglass.

He would especially like to thank Dr Michael Andrews, Albyn Austin, Rock Battye, John Broughton, Sarah Chaplin-Brice, Barbara Cowan, Michael Davies-Shiel, Douglas Ferreira, Peter Frost-Pennington, Michael Faulkner, Mary Hall, Geoffrey Holme, Richard Kirkman, Guy Moser, Barbara Newton, Gordon Nichol, Kenneth Norman, Peter Robinson, Raymond Sankey, Betty Smith, Edward Paget-Thomlinson, Michael Peascod, David Pickup, the Trustees of the Norman Nicholson Memorial Fund, Cliff Turner, Janet Woodhead and, not least for their forbearance, Heather and Kate van Zeller.

Readers will find more through the Record Offices at Barrow-in-Furness, Carlisle, Kendal and Whitehaven, the Cumbrian Railways Association, Eskdale Local History Society, the R&ER Heritage Group, and the following texts:

Davies: *The Ravenglass & Eskdale Railway* (Newton Abbott, 1968)
Kirkman & van Zeller: *Rails round the Cumbrian Coast* (Clapham, 1988)
Linton: *Handbook of the Whitehaven & Furness Junction Railway* (Whitehaven, 1851)
McGowan Gradon: *The Furness Railway* (Altrincham, 1946)
Melville & Hobbs: *Early Railway History in Furness* (Kendal, 1951)
Newton: *Ravenglass through the Ages* (Sellafield, 1989)
Orrell: *Around and About Ravenglass* (Ravenglass, 1976)
Parker: *The Gosforth District* (Whitehaven, 1922)
Turner: *Memories of Ravenglass* (Drigg, Holmrook, 1998)

Cumberland Pacquet
Cumbrian Railways, the Journal of the **Cumbrian Railways Association**
Transactions of the **Cumberland & Westmorland Antiquarian & Archaeological Society**
Whitehaven News

Published by The Cumbrian Railways Association,
a Registered Charity No. 1025436
www.cumbrian-rail.org
Membership Secretary, 36 Clevelands Avenue, Barrow-in-Furness, Cumbria. LA13 0AE

Design & layout by Michael Peascod,
104 Durley Avenue, Pinner, Middlesex, HA5 1JH
Printed by Lambert Print & Design, Settle, North Yorkshire.
ISBN 0-9519201-9-7

Introduction

Ravenglass is an ancient and small market town and seaport . . . It is built on the borders of a creek, near the confluence of the rivers Esk, Mite and Irt. The town, which is pleasantly situated along the seashore, consists principally of a long street of irregularly arranged dwellings - many of which are well built; the entire being sheltered in the background by the mountains of Black Combe. The adjacent country furnishes nothing for export . . . The harbour affords safe riding for vessels when put in by stress of weather.

(Slaters Directory 1848)

RAVENGLASS grew out of the sand where three rivers flow from the Cumbrian fells into the Irish Sea. Ancient beyond record, it was a natural site for people to live and travellers to journey through. Before the Roman fort, its medieval market place or the homes of the last three centuries were built, before main roads and rails were laid or England's first narrow-gauge train ran, this was *The Gateway to Paradise.*

For visitors and residents alike, it is a magical place. The first millennium of this small settlement is now so mysterious that its Roman name is uncertain and its Celtic legends forgotten, lost in time. The earliest written records date back only nine hundred years, but they show that a community was well established in 1208 when King John granted a Charter for the Fair. It remained largely independent of the Lord of nearby Muncaster, its parish church beyond the boundary of a deerpark that has constrained the growth of the Vil of Ra'nglass.

No greater in extent now than in medieval times, Ravenglass has one Main Street, enclosed but wide enough for a market, and a small modern housing estate on the old Town Fields, crammed between the tide-washed sands and the curve of George Stephenson's last main line railway. From the station yard, trains run into the Lakeland mountains on a scenic narrow-gauge route built over 125 years ago. The story of La'al Ratty, changed to a model size during a Great War and saved twice by railway enthusiasts, is serendipity itself.

For many people Ravenglass is synonymous with steam, but others come for walking, wildlife, sailing or simply to be there. Few places in the world are so little changed by the passage of time. The interesting question is - why?

Where legions marched into the Roman Fort, LMS ex-Midland Railway Compound 4-4-0 No.1021 of 1906 departs south from Ravenglass circa 1930, past the Customs Boat House and the town on the bank of the River Esk.

Photo: Mary Fair

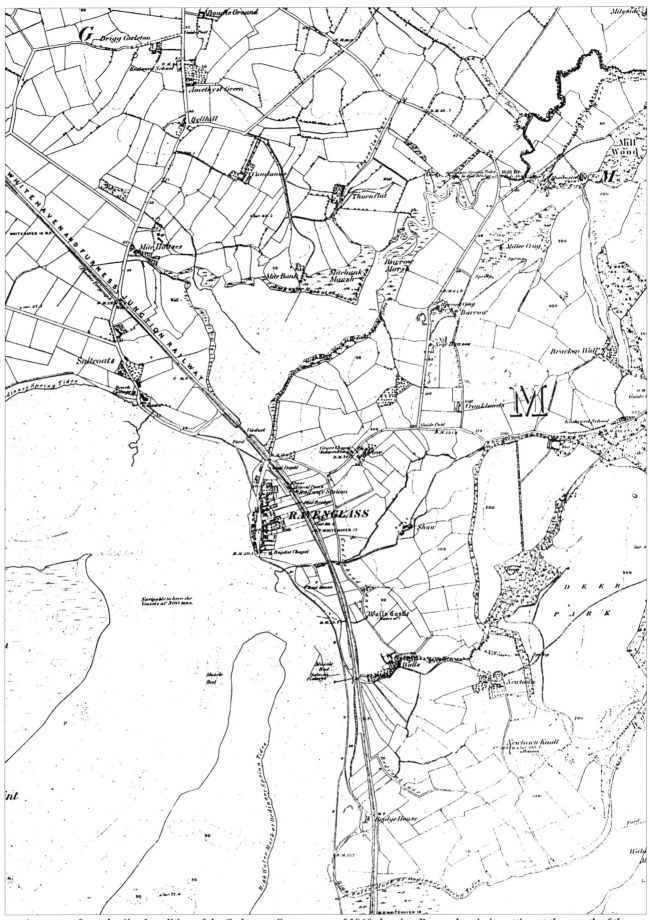

An extract from the 6in. 1st edition of the Ordnance Survey map of 1860 showing Ravenglass in its setting at the mouth of the River Mite.

1:

Before Recorded Time

This place was inhabited long before 'legal memory'

A timeless scene where galleys once beached between the fort and the port, at the foot of Hulot (later Town) Beck.
Photo: Sankey Collection

ACROSS the centuries from Stone Age to Lake District National Park, people from the greatest of society to slaves give us their names, their stories and many other clues to the history of this onetime port of Ravenglass.

Where the Cumbrian hills rise from the Irish Sea, travellers had to skirt the high ground or cross water nearby. But, with little agriculture, minerals or industry, this settlement barely grew from its first foundation before Roman times to the coming of the railways over 150 years ago. While so much of the world changed beyond recognition, the geography of Ravenglass did not.

Here three rivers, the Esk, Mite and Irt, drain into a land-locked estuary, a natural harbour facing the Isle of Man and a direct sail from Ireland or Wales. When first mapped, each river made its own way to sea before the sandy spits of Eskmeals and Drigg Point closed the Irt and Esk together, and strangled the haven.

These rivers run through rocks fractured aeons ago in volcanic uplift, granite foothills to Lakeland's highest peaks. The Esk was the Celtic *Water of Life.* The Mite, from an old word *to urinate,* has an intermittent flow from a spate to a trickle! Yet, before losing its headwaters to Eskdale in the much-changed climate of the past, this river cut a wide plain between the high ridges. Dug below sea level by glaciers, Wastwater dampens fluctuations in the Irt. Its steady flow could not keep the original estuary mouth open against the sand drifting along the shore.

In the dunes, the first trace of man was flint, chipped five thousand years ago before the sand-spits grew together. Later stone axes were quarried from Scafell and Langdale, then carried down the River Esk through the forest which covered all but the high peaks. Workers polishing tools had sand, seafood and a safe harbour on this coast. Traders steered their skin-covered craft for the great gap in the mountains to find landfall and the much-prized axeheads to barter in the islands or southern Britain.

From the Iron Age, haematite from Eskdale was smelted in hearths hereabouts, fuelled with wood being cleared from the hills. Because it was warmer throughout the year than the present, there were homes and fields on surrounding fells, with stone circles on Irton Pike and Burnmoor. On Barrow Brow, a promontory overlooking Ravenglass, ancient stone dikes enclose four acres of *The Great Round,* names which still recall those Celtic times.

The *Carvetii* were the dominant regional tribe in AD 79 when Roman troops moved to take North Britain into their Empire. Tacitus recorded that Governor Agricola led his 20th Legion with a fleet escort *aestuaria ac silvas ipse.* This estuary would be sheltered for galleys to berth. *Glanaventa*, the Latin name attributed by historians, suggests the Romans landed by a town on the riverbank. Perhaps its Celtic name survived: *yr Afon Glass* still translates from Welsh as *the Green River.*

Opposite the mouth of the Esk and above high tides of the time, the Romans built a marching camp. Its turf rampart was strengthened by timber when Emperor Hadrian made

A Place of Legends - King Eveling's Palace, Lyons Yards, Ulfson's Hospice, Walls - the remains of the Roman Bath House stand outside the perimeter ditch of the Hadrianic fort, beside fields rich in archaeological finds. Photo: Peter van Zeller

his northern frontier. Later, the perimeter was faced with sandstone brought from a distance. A Tribune commanded 500 men in barracks on this far flank of the Wall. Four miles up the Esk, a large kiln supplied roof tiles for buildings here and at other forts inland at Hardknott and Ambleside. Along roads only traceable in part, foreign conscripts held down a wild territory for mineral wealth and for grain grown on the outlying fells.

Outside the fort was the social centre of a bathhouse with pools and heating. This remains the tallest Roman building in the North, its thick walls buttressed for a vaulted roof, rendered in shell-lime mortar, with a niche for a statue. Close around were parade grounds, stockades and a civilian settlement, the *Vicus*, spreading some 400yds northwards. People fished, farmed, worked iron and traded with Celtic lands beyond the Imperial boundary. This was the last outpost of an Empire that stretched six thousand miles east and south.

To intercept raiders on the Solway or escort supplies from Caernarvon, the navy had *Pictae*, scout ships like curraghs, with twenty oarsmen in sea-green camouflage. In troop records, *First Cohort Morinii* from the Channel coast garrisoned Glanaventa, while *Cohort I Aelia Classica* left a lead seal, found in the excavations of 1977. Throughout the Roman occupation, this exposed flank needed protection as the region simmered with violence.

Black ash inside the fort is first dated around 197. A century later, the defences were destroyed and subsequently restored. Like the naval base at Holyhead they lay in the front line, and after the Picts invaded in 367 were rebuilt yet again. When troops withdrew to Rome a generation later, the land facing Ireland kept *Vigilia Maris* to protect its people. At this stronghold, *Sea Wake* was taxed and the bathhouse remained a high status building for another thousand years.

From these dark ages legends also endured: Saint Patrick captured as a boy by pirates, a great fleet sunk in Selker Bay, *King Eveling that heere had his court and roiall palace,* Arthur taking his journey to the nether regions from Lyons Garde. After the battle of Chester was lost in 613, the people of Wales were physically separated from the Cymri of *Rheged*. In Cumbria these Celts mainly inhabited the uplands, and new tribes colonised the wooded lowlands, a process still mapped today by the distinctive place-names around Ravenglass.

When Anglian settlers came to plough the heavier soils on the coastal plains, they cleared sites at *Irton* and *Santon*. The *Ceols* were workers on a royal estate at *Carlton*. A further distinction also survived the centuries: christianised by Irish monks, they raised carved stone crosses at places of worship. The earliest from a monastery around 800 stands 10ft tall outside Irton Church. At *Muncaster* near the old Roman camp, the Cross has the plaited motifs seen on the Isle of Man.

From there came Norsemen to shelter in this isolated land, but not the terror fighters cursed elsewhere. These Vikings had fled the Isles before a punitive raid by the King of Norway. They cut clearings in the forests at *Waberthwaite* and *Murthwaite,* keeping their mountain culture independent of England as native Prince Dunmail was defeated by King Edmund in 945. Cumbria then became part of Strathclyde under Malcolm King of Scots, *his ally by land or sea.* By Gosforth Cross, hogback stones carved with ranks of armed men record such events.

Archaeology does not yet reveal when Ravenglass was settled but it was a node in the maritime community of the Irish Sea, whatever its politics. Dragonhead longships used the Esk as a staging post in a trade network even wider than that of Rome. The river was a defensible border long after the Norman Conquest of England. The Domesday Survey of Yorkshire recorded *W'itingha, Bodele* and *Santacherche* (Whicham, Bootle and Kirksanton), but north was Scots land for a further century. When King Henry I founded a priory at Carlisle in 1102, Waldeive, son of Gospatrick, Earl of Dunbar and Baron of Allerdale gave to it . . . *other ancient buildings called Lyons Yards often remembered in that history of Arthur, the ruines whereof are yet to be seen . . . as it is thought at Ravenglass.*

2:

Ra'nglass in the Records

Medieval Ravenglass became a thriving market town

THE *Land of Carliol* was exchanged twice before the Normans became overlords of the Cumbri. They bought land in *Kaupeland* (the name literally means *bought land*) with power over body and soul. From the new castles and monasteries, their dealings survive *de jure et de facto*. In the reign of King Stephen, his son William of Lancaster granted the *vil of Mulcaster* to Furness Abbey, and about 1180, Gamel Lord of Pennington in Furness gave Conishead Priory the church by Muncaster Cross, still dedicated to *St Michael and All Saints*. Its first priest was Walter, but from 1220 to 1844 the church was under the Rectors of Waberthwaite.

Roger of Ra'nglas (written in abbreviated secretarial hand) gave the Priors two acres of land in the *vil of Ranglas . . . lying above the field called Croftonflet and Watelands, between the land of Richard Batewrit and Hubert Neuton, al the land of Editheknot.* Richard Robertson bequeathed *lands situated within these limits beginning where the Hulotbec falls on the sands, and up the bec to Aylicroft, from thence to Kirkstie, and along Kirkstie to the King's Road and along the great road to the south, till where it crosses Hulotbec.*

Here salt marsh was reclaimed and colonised. Accessible to ships as sea levels fell, the village around the Cross displays a medieval plan, narrow defensible entries to Main Street with side streets towards the Town Fields where the freemen had strips. A school was founded before the one at St Bees, whose Priors kept the hospice used by Scots pilgrims en route for Santiago. Edward Ulfson of Waberthwaite gave 20 acres of land *to a hospital I have made in Renglas for the accommodation of poor travellers and for the repair of the bridge I have made over the Esk.*

When Richard de Luci became Baron of Egremont in 1204, his forebear had been Justicier for King Henry II, the highest noble in the land. Lord Richard had a judicial review of the ancient customs of Copeland and services of its free tenants, before obtaining the first market charter in the Baronies of Cumberland. At *Kirkebi-in-Kendale* on 20 August 1208 King John granted, for the annual gift of a saddle horse, a Royal Charter to a Saturday Market and a Fair each year at his Manor of Ra'nglas.

Held in high summer on the Feast of St James with its link to Compostella, the Fair began with a great procession from Bell Hill across the River Mite to Ravenglass Cross. After a proclamation by the Lord's Steward, the Serjeants of the Bow of Egremont, his foresters and all his tenants bound to attend, swore to *protect merchandise against freebooters and a foreign enemy*, paid dues to their lord and enjoyed his hospitality in free ale and feasting.

Baron de Luci also concluded an agreement of 1 December 1208 about *the whole land and fee of Renglas*. Alan de Penitone could sublet *Gaurestal and Moldcorkin* for 10s to William, grandson of Edward Ulfson, and thence to Roger of Renglas. For one twelfth of a knight's fee and foreign military service due to the King, Alan held the family *tenement of Mulecaster*, but Ravenglass was beholden to Lord Egremont. They were to keep cattle off each other's land, while Richard had rights to take timber from anywhere in Alan's manor but the boundary of *Bereghillebank*, to build a fishgarth in the Esk.

This was the *Monkgarth*, while there were soon fishtraps on the Mite and *Hirt* (sic) with *the saltpits of Eskc* and Saltcoats nearby. Herrings here *lye in sholes together so thike in the sea at spawning, about August, as a ship cannot pass throw; and the fishers go from all the coast.* Among donors to St Bees Priory in 1240 *Yvo Faber* was no common smith but one of the wealthy in the iron trade. From a pound above the old Roman bathhouse, water long powered such industry; centuries later his forge (*Budir* in Norse) had been anglicised in name to Butter Mill.

As its trade grew, when Edward I took Scotland from William Wallace, the Bailiffs of Ravenglass were ordered to send ships to Winchelsea by Midsummer Day 1297 to face war in France. In 1324 this Port of Egremont was among a hundred in the land ordered to prepare for the King's service any ship measured to carry over 40 tuns. Over 800 years ago, it was a place of some importance.

The medieval village settled on the shore, protected from storm tides with masonry robbed from the Roman fort. The Ship Inn guarded the Great Road to the south. Beyond old mooring posts, the ford and the railway to the north cross the River Mite.
Photo: Peter van Zeller

Main Street spreads out around the old market place where the Charter Fair was held each year from 1209. The distant figures indicate the original central position of the mediaeval cross and its relocation in 1774. On the left, Clifton Terrace has the oldest house in the village, dated 1689. Photo: Author's Collection.

Ravenglass.

Walter de Mulcaster was first Member of Parliament for Cumberland, when slaves like Simon White were given to the Prior of St Bees by Alan de Pennington *for the salvation of his soul*. To resist the raids from Scotland, the family had moved to Muncaster about 1242, a *new Town . . . built for the better convenience and security of the inhabitants*, but were fined by King Edward II for raising battlements on the Pele Tower. Here King Henry VI presented a glass goblet, *The Luck of Muncaster*. He took refuge after losing the Battle of Hexham on 14 May 1464 and Chappels now marks the place where he was found.

A manorial watermill was first recorded in 1455 at Muncaster Mill, the closest place to the sea where the River Mite had enough fall to power an overshot wheel. On the fell above there were tentergrounds for the woollen industry. Two miles inland where there was fulling at Walk Mill, a jury settled the disputed *Right of Mill* between the Penningtons and Irtons in 1557.

Growing wealth from Kendal's cloth trade is seen in the Commonplace Book of John Pennington, Sheriff of Cumberland, in 1500. On St James' Day he took rents from tenants, while his 1700 *old schepe* gave 5 packs of wool and over 600 lambs. His income was over £200 a year, more than the local religious houses and a quarter of Furness Abbey itself. At the Dissolution of Monasteries, his brother William held both the Manor of Muncaster from the Percys, who were now Lords of Egremont, and also, for an additional *17th part of a knight's fee, homage, fealty and the puture of two serjeants . . . the hamlet of Ravenglass.*

Percy tenants had *common of pasture in Moulcastre Fell, for a boon day to the Lords of Moulcastre in harvest . . . in braken time . . . for graving and another for bearing of peats.* Ten households also had licence *to Lode and unlode at the fare tyme, called Sayncte Jame's tyde . . . severall vessells called Pickerdes of the burden of ix or ten tunne . . . the Awners whereof is Walter Cadye, William Cadye, William Coupland and Nicholas Harbet, and their partners, whose common trade is to go to Chester, Leverpoole and those Coasts with Cariage of heringes and to bye Sallte. Ships of thre or four score tons may come in on a full sea at spring tide* as reported to Queen Elizabeth I to *prevent piracy and smuggling.*

For centuries the Penningtons had iron mines in Egremont and Furness. In 1636 they went into partnership to build a waterwheel driving bellows and tilt hammer at Forgehills near Muncaster Head. Though the iron ore in Eskdale was surrounded by woods coppiced for charcoal, production demanded that more ore had to be brought in. Soon not *one tree in sixty in the district stood above eight ft high . . . and 40 Tenauntes of Eshdall and Miterdall* petitioned *this wastfull and uncharitable burneinge* would force them to live *in rockes through want of Houssies.*

As this iron fed the arsenals of Civil War, Sir John Pennington was a bold Lord High Admiral to King Charles I. Later during Richard Cromwell's Protectorate, William Thompson, yeoman farmer of Thornflatts and County Magistrate, judged on misdemeanours against Puritanism: *fulling on the Lord's day . . . swearing oaths . . . drinking on 26th December 1658 . . .* and a fracas in Muncaster Church caused by two visiting Quakers!

In a re-enactment of the Wars of the Roses when King Henry VI fled here, the Yorkist pennant flies outside Muncaster Castle. The castle's defensive position was strategically sited from Roman times, on the Scottish border after the Norman Conquest, and still overlooks the lowest bridging point of the River Esk. Photo: Peter van Zeller

3:

Restoration & Rebuilding

Modern Ravenglass took shape but went into decline

With the Restoration of King Charles II, whose Vice-Admiral was Sir William Pennington, *Ravenglass had but a little market but a great fair at St James' Tyde both for cattle from Ireland and Ile of Man and other and our own country comodities.* Many houses in Main Street would then be like *the Old Thack,* until a Great Rebuilding began. No.1 Clifton Terrace has *1689* on its heart-shaped stone as the oldest dated home of the modern village - the year that Edward Stanley of Eskdale declared for King William of Orange.

In 1695 a company *for the Pearl-Fishing in this river - lately something of a Bubble* - found £800 of *Shell-berries* in local oysters. More enduring was the £100 endowment of Richard Brockbank, cook at Muncaster Castle, for *a Master to teach a free school.* The School was founded in Town Lane by 26 April 1706, but, by about 1740, parents tried to remove its master, Thomas Booth. *The children never the better by going to him* had the adventure of the sea around.

Cottages on the present Village Green were named *Gibraltar Row* after spoils of the War of Spanish Succession. When Christopher Woodall was Mayor of Ravenglass, a sailor returned from the Porto Bello raid to avenge Jenkin's Ear, and lost his medal at the Roman fort! Nearby was the boathouse from where the Customs cutter swept out on Coastwaiter duties. The Running Trade from the Isle of Man was rife in 1758 when Preventive Officer Herbert and his men seized contraband tea and spirits, then were themselves attacked by 22 armed smugglers, some dressed as women!

From here trains of packhorses followed tracks over the fells. In 1750 Parliament had approved a turnpike project from Calder Bridge through Ravenglass to Duddon Bridge, but nothing happened to ease delays to travellers waiting at Crosswater or to ford the Mite. John Wesley warned of *a generation of liars, who detain all strangers as long as they can, either for their own gain or their neighbours.* Among the buildings improved from those profits, *Lorne Cottage* has a *1762* datestone, *The Bay Horse* one of *1766*, while *Pennington House* has a fine Georgian frontage.

The Fair continued, although the Cross was rebuilt to the side of Main Street in 1774. Its new sandstone pillar, octagonal with a conical top, cost 6s 6d. People came from across the county with horses, cattle or wool, and there were up to 45 booths. However, receipts barely covered the cost of the traditional ale and cake for tenants of Lord Egremont *riding the Fair*, the tollers' wages and *Music and Scales*.

Sir John Pennington obtained a new charter in 1775 for three one-day fairs and a weekly market from which Irish cattle were sold for droving to the cities. As 1st Baron Muncaster he promoted agricultural improvements and prospected for iron ore in the deerpark. He contributed much to the modern landscape by rebuilding the Castle with its lodge of 1781, improving the drainage of fields, and planting new hedges and woodlands around them.

Alas, there were now few ships trading or building here; in 1736 the *Cumberland* cost Sir James Lowther and Captain Walter Lutwidge £ 2,500. However the 66ft *Mary* launched at Ravenglass in 1742 needed over 12ft to float and had to trade from Whitehaven. With rum, coal and railways from pit to quay, this port was now one of the busiest in the kingdom, after being secondary to Ravenglass. Here the population was in decline, and by 1791 there were only half the marriages and births there had been two hundred years before.

Although the Esk was still navigable four miles upstream, the marshes were silting. Early maps show separate river mouths, but by 1770 Elliot drew the Irt flowing south into the *Trident of the Irish Channel* (seen by Samuel Coleridge from the summit of Scafell in 1802). A buoy was moored in the estuary, but when it broke loose, the cost of repair was not met by the 8d harbour dues. Indeed, some captains refused to pay a fee when there was only an open roadstead. There was firm sand to anchor in the deepwater channel and posts that ships could moor against, awaiting a floodtide to get close to the village. Here they beached for carts to load alongside.

In 1800 the Agent proposed harbour improvements to Lord Muncaster, but nothing happened until after a public meeting held at Whitehaven in 1822. Voluntary subscriptions funded a stone tower on the Knott. Lawson's chart shows a beacon in the dunes as leading mark to find the passage. However there was now only one 39ft sloop *Duchess of Leinster* belonging to the port and trade was *relatively trifling! St Jame Fair was* the *Largest assembly of drunken beggars and fortune tellers ever assembled,* when the Manor Court fined Chrispin Pharoah of Eskdale a shilling for *not attending at Ravenglass Fair* in 1815.

James Lawson's Chart was published to revive navigation into the combined estuary of the Rivers Esk, Mite and Irt. It shows a beacon and a tall tower on Newtown Knott, newly erected in 1823 to guide ships displacing up to 300 tons across the bar.
Chart: Transactions of the C&WAAS

Opposite the Ship Inn was the last house of pre-restoration Ravenglass. The Old Thack, where boatman Joe Farren and his son Pat lived before it was demolished in 1923 to allow a direct drive from Main Street to Mountain Ash and Rose Cottage. Photo: Author's Collection

Daniel's *Voyage round Gt. Britain* found *a dirty, ragged, forlorn looking town which in its own wretchedness and the dreariness of its situation may be pronounced the most miserable place in the kingdom . . . no great discoverer has yet adverted to the convenience of a ferry boat, though with every tide there is someone to feel the need of it. There is a wooden bridge over the Mite, designed by a native engineer, and built so as to be of as little use as possible, being so low that it is passable only when the tide is out and the river fordable!*

A local committee convened by Lord Muncaster finally secured a bridge over the River Esk near to the sea, *In consequence of repeated complaints from the Post Office that the mail gigs which run between Ulverston and Ravenglass and between Ravenglass and Whitehaven do not perform their respected duties in the allotted time.* Nicknamed after its builders, *The Wrestlers' Bridge* took great endeavour by the Dixon brothers of Grasmere. The keystone was laid with ceremony on 25 June 1829 and still stands under the main A595. The mailcart ran 3 times a week before being briefly overtaken by the *Princess Royal* coach to Ulverston which still took the shore road *if tides permitted.*

Ravenglass had four inns, four boot makers, two tailors, carpenters, surgeons, a grocer, and a linen and wool draper. Then in 1836 came prescience that steam trains would soon link London and Scotland. While the Grand Junction Railway sent engineer Joseph Locke to find a route over Shap Fell, Sir Humphrey le Fleming Senhouse of Seascale Hall invited Old George Stephenson himself to make *an Ocular Survey* around the Cumbrian coast.

Below : The 1st Ordnance Survey map published in 1860 shows a row of cottages in Town Lane, now occupied by Townfield Close, the original railway station and single track main line.

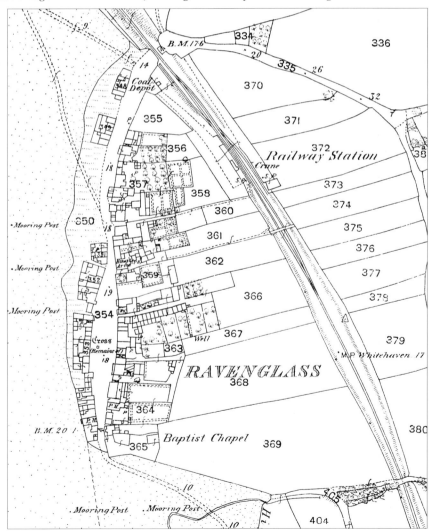

4:

Main Line to Nowhere

The Whitehaven & Furness Junction Railway opened to Ravenglass in 1849

THE Father of Railways proposed a level route through Ravenglass by the present alignment, but crossing the Duddon sands and Morecambe Bay direct to Lancaster so that a *new small county of England* could be reclaimed. The West Cumberland Railway went to Parliament with more revolutionary ideas by John Hague and John Rastrick. Alas, its aim to be the main line to Scotland was scotched by the government-favoured route over Shap. Sir Humphrey went to command the Far East Fleet, but died of fever in 1841 as Hong Kong was seized; his memorial, a Chinese bell, still hangs in Gosforth church.

When the Whitehaven Junction Railway arrived in that port from the north, a new company was formed to go south. The Whitehaven & Furness Junction (W&FJR) would link to the Furness Railway (FR), opened in 1846, for access to steamers to Fleetwood. Alas, the W&FJ Extension Railway conflicted with shipping rights into creeks like Greenodd, and was spoiled by schemes to join the Kendal & Windermere or the Lancaster & Carlisle Railways. Shareholders objected that money was wasted on plans *to the stoppage of business on the original line.*

Surveys were completed under superintendence of George Stephenson. His son Robert was engineer-in-charge, the most experienced in the world, who was also planning the Chester & Holyhead Railway with its Britannia Bridge, and the East Coast line crossing Tyne and Tweed. He gave the Directors *utterances of unabashed confidence,* but when, short of funds, the W&FJR decided to hug the coast and link with the FR near Broughton, construction was left to resident engineer James Dees, Michael Longridge of the Furness and contractors Brotherton & Rigg. Leaving Whitehaven the navvies crossed bogs by laying hurdles, then moved a million cubic yards of spoil on the 16¾ miles to Ravenglass. A double line formation was made, but only one track was laid, with timber sleepers and iron rails linked in special chairs. Men were still pile-driving on the embankments when the first goods train set off.

On 26 February 1849 a Whitehaven Junction Railway loco ran to Sellafield. Beyond here Brown & Richardson's men were completing timber trestle viaducts across the Rivers Ehen, Calder, Irt and Mite. Seawalls and bridges were being faced with sandstone from the beach by Nethertown. The first two W&FJR locomotives were delivered from Newcastle and pushed through the streets of Whitehaven on temporary tracks, sadly running over a local jeweller with fatal results. The public opening on 19 July 1849 was described in the Cumberland Pacquet:

Nine first, second and third class carriages . . . three additional goods waggons filled up with seats . . . attached to a new and powerful engine . . . a band of music had been engaged livening the proceedings with a number of appropriate tunes. The weather proved somewhat unfavourable . . . a heavy shower pouring down at the time of setting out but this did not dampen the ardour . . . and the cheering of the large throng. The long train glided away easily and rapidly down the valley of St Bees in gallant and majestic trim. The train arrived at Ravenglass some twenty minutes before two, where the party was welcomed by the inhabitants. A handsome and bountiful collation had been provided by order of the Directors for their numerous guests, in a capacious building of wood, erected as a shelter for the carriages and goods. This was served in excellent style by Mr Whinneray, the worthy host of the Kings Arms, and consisted of a plentiful supply of the most substantial viands and an abundance of nut brown ale and bottled porter.

A pretty triumphant arch of evergreens swayed over the opening ceremony of the Whitehaven & Furness Junction Railway held on 19 July 1849 at Ravenglass and on 1 November 1850 at Broughton-in-Furness. Illustrated London News

The *roomy and commodious* station, 150yds beyond the road bridge at Ravenglass, had a loop, two sidings, *engine and goods sheds, booking office, wharf, platforms and depots. The coal and lime depots are in connection with the girder bridge and form a fine entrance from the north to the town.*

After opening, there were three trains on weekdays, two on Sundays. Only a month later *an excellent well built second hand Post Coach was* auctioned in Whitehaven. Now travel was available to all. First class tickets cost 3s 6d, but in the first year over half the 71,618 passengers went third class at 1s 5d. More than 500 people took cheap trips to the newly revived Ravenglass Fair where there was *dancing at all 3 inns until the early hours.*

For twelve months this was the operating base, where a loco stabled overnight. Extending the line south cut through the site of the Roman fort where a coin of Vespasian and three underground chambers were found 15ft deep and 12ft in diameter holding human bones, two oak clubs and a shoe. Building embankments to reduce the crossing of the River Esk to a still lengthy 330yd cost wagon driver Haynes his leg, caught by a wheel.

Then, the night after the 36 spans had passed inspection by Captain Wynne, a great fire burned part of the *noble viaduct of timber* down to the water. The navvies who had heated tar to protect the trestles swore they had not been smoking and that they had put their brazier out the night before! It cost £600 to repair. Hence the opening to Bootle on 8 July 1850 was only marked by a simple note on timetables about the new coach connections to the south.

After final inspection by Lt Douglas Colton RE (*excellent style of every department*), the opening to Broughton-in-Furness on 1 November 1850 was a great occasion. The official special from Whitehaven arrived by an arch of greenery and flags alongside a train from Furness for a feast at *The Old King's Head*, all drawn by an artist from the Illustrated London News. The navvies meantime, *a fine body of men well attired*, had their own celebration marching in procession from Bootle Station.

While rails were not to link Furness with the rest of Lancashire for seven years, the W&FJR was also isolated at Whitehaven. Here wagons were moved through the streets on carts. A priority to dig a tunnel proved difficult through the unstable ground under the park around Lord Lonsdale's Whitehaven Castle. In 1853 Parliament approved *Branch Tramways to the harbours at Whitehaven and Ravenglass which may become essential for the traffic of the company.* From the cutting through the Roman fort, a siding was to lead 291yds onto a pier in the estuary where ships of 300 tons could anchor. However funds had now run out and only the branch through Whitehaven Market was ever completed. Six ships used Ravenglass in 1854, but the port was in final decline.

From 1851 William Phizackla was Stationmaster at Ravenglass. For 15s a week, he handled *the principal articles of export - hoops, cockles, mussels and salmon.* Outside his office were two signals. When the single line was first operated on time-interval, the service was notorious for economy and poor timekeeping, especially when Jonathan Harker the guard ran cockfights at intermediate stations! After the electric telegraph was connected, his colleague at St Bees was found both drunk on duty and not able to understand the system when sober!

Following pooling with the Whitehaven Junction, W&FJR locos achieved notable reliability, running 190 miles a day. Distinctive in dark green paint with classical names on brass plates, they had extra buffers for shunting mineral wagons. When the Furness linked with the Ulverstone & Lancaster Railway in 1857, the W&FJR became a main line at last. Through trains were provided with footwarmers and the services of a conductor guard. The Directors immediately bought him a new watch! With higher running speeds of 40mph, he reported the alarming swaying of the Esk viaduct. Boards instructing *Shut Off Steam were* put up, and then extra wrought iron ties fitted to stiffen the timbers. However the once isolated line now started to make steady profits and could face the need for the regular renewal of bridge timbers and sleepers.

The discovery of iron ore at Hodbarrow revived Whitehaven plans to cut across Furness. The FR also proposed to bridge the Duddon to secure its growing town and new port of Barrow from being by-passed, but Parliament decided on the W&FJR scheme. So the Furness Railway took it over with a guaranteed 8% dividend on the shares. Iron columns were cast and a trackbed begun near Askam, before the direct crossing was abandoned in 1891. Ravenglass would remain *in the back settlements.*

The earliest known photograph of a Whitehaven & Furness Junction Railway local mixed train. Southward bound through Eskmeals Station after the Furness Railway takeover in 1865, 0-6-0 locomotive No.42 (formerly W&FJR No.19 Lonsdale), was recovered from its plunge onto the main road at Ravenglass to run fifty years in service!
Photo: Cumbrian Railways Association Collections

5:

Furness Railway take-over

The Whitehaven line was transformed

The splendid new Furness Railway station buildings date from 1873. The elevated signalbox gave clear sightlines to both ends of the loop alongside the double track, to enable the reversal of short working passenger trains.

Photo: From the collection of Mr. A.D. Smith

SOON after the Furness Railway take-over, Ravenglass saw a local crisis on 11 August 1866. Around 10.30am the Foxfield Luggage train was put into the Coal Depot to allow two other trains to pass, *a rather unusual occurance,* as the timetable was evidently some two hours adrift! When ex-W&FJR 0-6-0 No.19 *Lonsdale* finally set off for Whitehaven after shunting back out of the siding, the crew did not reset the hand worked point which was propped open. *The next moment, the standing truck, tender, engine, one wagon and two trucks fell over the end of the siding on to the highway, the distance of the fall being some twenty feet.* The three men on the footplate were scalded and a wagonload of sheep escaped. A strong travelling crane with a long length of temporary track was needed to get the loco back onto the permanent way!

The congestion of the long single line could only get worse with the construction of the route from Egremont to Sellafield, while the existing track and long timber bridges needed urgent attention. The Esk viaduct was rebuilt first, with massive sandstone piers begun on 1 February 1867 and completed with riveted wrought iron lattice girders the following summer. Engineer Charles Timmins continued in like manner to replace the timber trestles across the Mite and Irt by June 1868 at a total cost of £23,572.

Both formation and viaducts were now wide enough for a double line. James Hunter & Co already maintained the FR track and started to lay new steel rails alongside in May 1871. The first section of extra track was completed from Bootle to Ravenglass and Drigg on 26 April 1872. The navvies under Resident Engineer John Thomson were

mostly south country, big men and good workers, but very fond of their beer . . . if not near a pub, there was a barrel kept in the brake van, and a man to give the beer out!

Following the accident the station had both points and signals fully interlocked in one of the earliest signal boxes on the Furness system. This was manned by George Glaister, from 5.45am to 9.50pm in summer and 8.00am to 6.00pm in winter, but closed on Sundays. It had an 18-lever Easterbrook frame, and Tyers 3-position instruments for block working on the double tracks. It was unusually elevated on a granite plinth to give clear sight of the running tracks. The lower quadrant semaphores all had wooden posts on which the oil lamps were raised by winch.

To complete the improvements, the station with its simple hut on a low platform also needed rebuilding, as the Duke of Devonshire explained to shareholders in 1875:

On the Whitehaven section especially some of the stations were of most inferior description and such as the Board of Trade would not have them continue. They were temporary structures scarcely more than wooden hovels and it was absolutely necessary to lay out a good deal of money in improving them.

Lancaster architects Paley & Austin designed many attractive Furness buildings of the day. Like Drigg and Bootle, the plan seen earlier at Greenodd and Haverthwaite was followed here, with red sandstone mouldings and walls of local pink granite. Ravenglass uniquely had a narrow platform awning, while the stationmaster's house, waiting rooms and booking hall had fine details like rainwater hoppers cast *18 FR 73.* Opposite was a standard Furness goods shed with elegant round arched windows and

Ravenglass

buttresses like a small church. Pencilled in the south elevation of the plans, but not built, was a second portico for road wagons. In the goods yard beyond were a cattle dock, small crane and weigh house.

The new Stationmaster, Thomas Hesketh, came from Cheshire; his son was clerk, with two porters, Thomas Phizacklea and Daniel Steel, as befitted the community's main link with the outside world. The timetable was still sparse, with three stopping trains each way and an extra on Thursdays when farmers' wives took produce to Whitehaven Market. But from 1875 the *Carnforth & Whitehaven Sorting Tender* took mail for return from London overnight! 1892 saw a lineside collection point listed for the *Up Limited Travelling Post Office* but this was soon changed for nets by the northbound track.

On the staggered Up platform stood a timber waiting shelter painted dark brown and light buff with windows in white. Over the roadbridge strengthened in 1880, this platform was later carried on iron columns (like those once cast for the Duddon viaduct) at a cost of £150 in 1895. Any hope of reducing the long journey south was lost with the routeing of most trains through Barrow Central but the isolation of the coastline brought its own reward.

On 2 April 1898 a new branch tramway was completed to the gun testing range of Vickers Son & Maxim, in the Eskmeals dunes. The thump of armaments, especially for the warships built at Barrow, was to be a familiar sensation in Ravenglass for the next century. There were periods when a halt for workmen was used at Monk Moors but otherwise local workers had passes to walk over the Esk

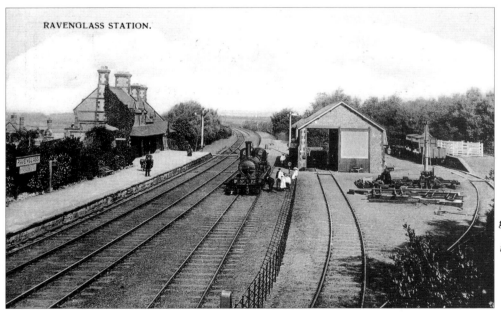

RAVENGLASS STATION.

The view north from the footbridge beside the Furness Railway signalbox shows an early Sharp, Stewart 0-6-0 about to shunt the yard for the roadside goods on a summer morning. The fifty-five 'Sharpies' were the most numerous FR class, and worked many different duties.
Photo: Cumbrian Railways Association Collections

viaduct. In 1911 this was strengthened with new steel plate centre girders at a cost of £25,000.

Of the W&FJR locos taken into Furness stock, the errant 0-6-0 *Lonsdale* lasted on local goods until 1910, but painted like FR locos in haematite red livery. All seven passenger trains then stopped at Ravenglass, with through coaches onto the Midland Railway for Leeds and London St Pancras and the London & North Western from Liverpool and Euston. The 8.17pm from Whitehaven terminated here and the following 9.14pm ran to the Windermere branch. There were roadside pickup goods and fast goods which called *to attach Workington Fish or Barrow Urgent Goods, Carnforth Fish and Foreign Empties Only.* The last Down train of the day was nicknamed *The Whip.*

This panorama of the village on 6 September 1894 would remain largely unchanged for another century, apart from the loss of the Smithy and Gibraltar Row, and the tower on Newtown Knott.
Sketch: Author's Collection, from the estate of Billy Wilson

A new industry, Tourism, was promoted with railway guides, circular tours and a special Ravenglass postcard by Heaton Cooper. The highlights of local operations included special trains and coaches for exalted guests at the Castle when Lord Muncaster was a long serving Board member and briefly chairman of the Furness Railway Company. The Royal Train was sometimes stabled overnight in the long headshunt, only distantly remembered now as *Queen's Siding.* The effect on the village was profound.

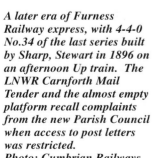

A later era of Furness Railway express, with 4-4-0 No.34 of the last series built by Sharp, Stewart in 1896 on an afternoon Up train. The LNWR Carnforth Mail Tender and the almost empty platform recall complaints from the new Parish Council when access to post letters was restricted.
Photo: Cumbrian Railways Association Collections

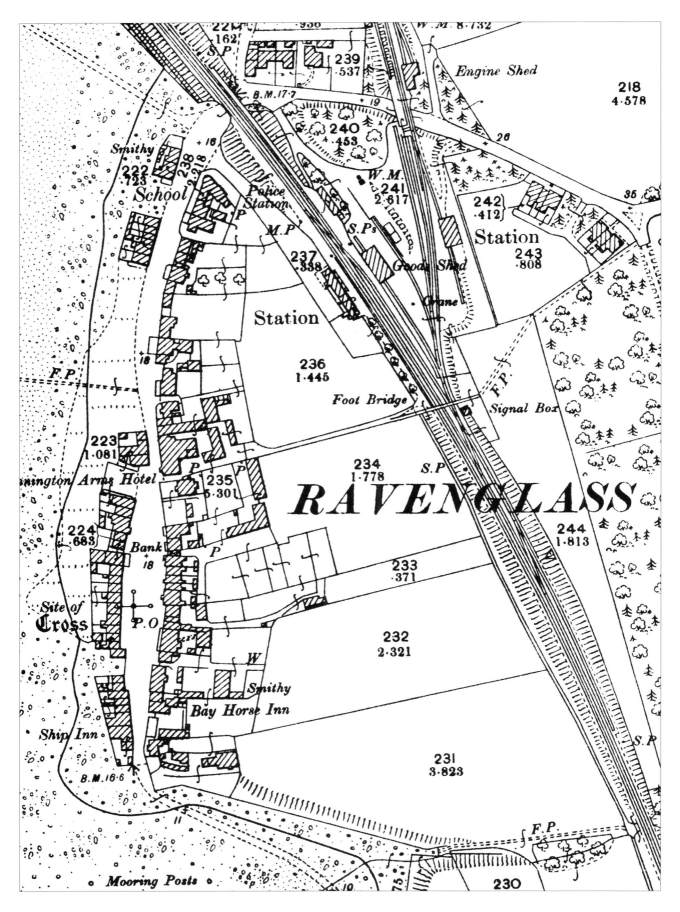

The second edition Ordnance Survey shows Ravenglass in 1899 with the main line standard gauge tracks as they existed from the 1870s until the 1960s, and the simple 3ft. gauge track layout.

6:

The Victorian Village

The idyll of a troubled man would endure for another century

PLANS in Parliament after 1839 reveal Ravenglass linked to the past. Behind Main Street with its Workhouse newly emptied to Bootle, there were tumbledown cottages in Back Lane, orchards and a Baptist Chapel. Narrow fields, not enclosed until 1842, stretched to Croftshead Lane, now Walls Drive. Iron ore yards promised development but, unlike nearby Barrow, this fishing hamlet remained sequestered. Indeed revolutionary writer and engraver William Linton came seeking its very isolation. He moved to Miteside, before it was extended by its new owner Willie Salmon.

When the W&FJR first opened, Jonathan Whinneray enlarged the *Kings Arms Inn*. Little then changed for a generation, until in 1876 Sir Josslyn Pennington purchased the entire Kings Arms Estate, a swath of land from the Mill to the Esk, the Butchers' barns and much of Main Street for a huge sum of £7,000. The old Inn was renamed the *Muncaster*, then the *Pennington Arms*, as Ravenglass became a model Garden Village to complement changes around the Castle. Here Anthony Salvin had added a tower and staterooms for Lord Gamell in 1860-4, and from the new rhododendron gardens, John Ruskin saw Eskdale as *The Gateway to Paradise*.

Before taking up residence, Sir Josslyn's own Greek Tragedy was the death of a friend in a kidnapping near Marathon, when he and his wife escaped. This international crisis was remembered for posterity in 1873 by the rebuilding of St Michael's Church, with its pre-Raphaelite windows by Holman Hunt. To relieve *This Great Sorrow*, Lord Muncaster funded social architecture around the park: Wells Cottages and municipal buildings by Station Hill, Police House, Infant and Church School, and House with *1878* datestone. The Public Hall *in the Swiss style* saw services and dances under the tall vaulted roof, Clifton Terrace was rebuilt, while the Working Men's Institute of 1898 had 40 members and over 700 volumes in its Reading Room.

In 1881 the Baron led excavations of the Burnmoor stone circle, an encampment at Devoke, and the fort and bathhouse at Ravenglass. Finds included the hypocaust and a stone with Roman letters which an illiterate labourer threw in the sea! Alas, some other ancient sites disappeared when the outlying crofts were unified into one Home Farm. The village cross was removed by Henry Lightfoot of Cranklands, and a pillar re-erected by Walls Mansion, completed in 1885. The last traditions of Market and Fair with Trotting Derby, wrestling and blindfold wheelbarrow races ceased before the new century, as the Sports simply became part of Muncaster Flower Show. A gentle kindly man, Sir Josslyn chaired the new Parish Council from 1894 and took a keen interest in *his* village from clearing rubbish to providing fireworks for Queen Victoria's Golden Jubilee celebration. Without a direct heir, his last testament simply willed *there should always be a Pennington at Muncaster to treasure its Luck*.

Meanwhile the village avoided real growth. Between the bridges besides the station yard, Railway Terrace was built where engine driver John Chapman lived. But there is a map of October 1886 for a *Ravenglass Building Estate* each side of the main line north of the Mite viaduct. Planned by *TL Banks & Townsend of London & Whitehaven* were no less than 66 new terraced homes, 12 semis and 10 detached villas, laid out with parkland walks and a promenade drive around a *Proposed Salt water Lake and* a footbridge across the river. As Seascale offered ready returns to the Furness Railway with seaside pier, bathing machines and golf course, so the Estate came to nothing.

While Barrow grew from a village of 200 people into *the English Chicago*, this very similar location was transfixed. The County Road Surveyor declared local roads *the worst kept and of least importance of any I have yet examined . . . interrupted by the tide at Ravenglass and Eskmeals*. Yet they were still used, notably by the elephants of circuses visiting Whitehaven. In 1853, six ships had loaded flour, oysters, bacon, potatoes and coal. In 1876 a lone schooner took iron ore for Newport and the first screw steamer landed stores for a merchant at Gosforth.

The new Police House, Infants School and Muncaster Parish Hall in the early 1900s, after the removal of the Smithy beside the ford across the River Mite, but before the demolition of Gibraltar Row Cottages.
Photo: Author's Collection

By 1910 the railway had sealed the final decline of the port. A Down Fast Goods steams towards Whitehaven behind FR No.7, a mixed-traffic 0-6-0 designed by Pettigrew and built in 1899 by the North British Loco Co.

Photo: Mary Fair

Whatever may have been the former importance of Ravenglass as a seaport, it is now quite deserted save by an occasional manure laden sloop in spring. Men dragged the mussel beds or looked for pearls undisturbed. Joe Farren the Boatman drew the salmon garth twice daily or rowed visitors to the Gulleries, where eggs were collected for market in London. Ashburners of Barrow sent the last commercial vessel Isabella *in 1914. This annual visit over, the bay was empty for the first period in its history.*

The smell of bird droppings surrounds the last commercial sailing ship beached on the hard. The brig Isabella *unloads its cargo of guano fertiliser for William Wilson to cart away in May 1914.*

Photo: Cumbrian Railways Association Collections

The Old Rat Trod

England's first public narrow gauge railway opened in 1875

Almost brand new. **0-6-0T** Devon *glistens in the afternoon sun after the arrival of the 3.10pm train in spring 1880, with the recently-completed Wells Cottages behind the original Ravenglass & Eskdale Railway station.*

Photo: National Railway Museum Collection

THE extraordinary expansion of Barrow-in-Furness affected the whole region. Its haematite iron and steel were profitable beyond measure, but closed to outside investors when one speculator, Faithfull Cookson, bought mineral rights to the Lake District mountains from Ennerdale to Eskdale in 1867, ripe for *Puffing* to swindle investors. In 1871 France lost the iron mines of Lorraine to Germany. As prices rose, Cookson floated a Whitehaven Iron Mines Limited. This planned several railways in the district - narrow gauge above Ennerdale, but standard gauge from Ravenglass with a link under the main line to a pier, a route to Nab Gill mine at Boot in Eskdale more direct than at present, and a branch up Miterdale. Yet the projected cost of £90,000 was far beyond its means.

Instead, an Act was passed in 1873 for the Ravenglass & Eskdale Railway (R&ER) to build the first public narrow-gauge line in England. Funded jointly by the Iron Mines Company and by contractor Ambrose Oliver, the seven-mile track was laid to 3ft gauge like many schemes of the day abroad. 50 navvies cut along the lie of the land up steep grades and round sharp bends by Muncaster Fell. Most of the roadbed was finished in 1874, so the contractor's loco could work trains to *King of Prussia bridge*. However, a long dispute with the Sharpe family at Spout House delayed completion to Boot until Manning, Wardle 0-6-0T *Devon was* ready. Named after the chairman of the two companies, this loco hauled its first goods train with iron ore, hoops and bobbins on 27 May 1875.

The R&ER now sought to carry passengers, but the Board of Trade Inspector, Col Yolland, found *nameboards, clocks, conveniences missing* and had never seen *masonry of such indifferent quality . . . that by reason of the incompleteness of the works . . . the opening of the Ravenglass and Eskdale Railway for traffic cannot be sanctioned without danger to the public!* The embankment around Rock Point was widened by 25ft before a further successful Inspection. On 20 November 1876, the opening train *gaily decorated with flags* started at 8.35am with Lord Muncaster riding on the engine. *It is hoped this little enterprise will bring a large number of visitors to the truly beautiful valley of the Esk. The district was quite en fête!*

Alongside the FR station yard, the narrow-gauge sidings at Ravenglass allowed trains to be shunted by gravity alongside a tall timber train-shed, with office and platform inside. Another line led to the brink of an overhead ore chute above the standard gauge. The tracks crossed the main road by two iron girder bridges, passing a stone engine shed with room inside for a second long-funnelled 0-6-0 tank loco named *Nabb Gill!*

The raised transhipment siding was incomplete when the contractor pushed the railway company into receivership only six months after the first passenger trains began operating. In Eskdale the line ran near the foot of inclined railways at Fisherground and Nab Gill mine, but ore traffic did not flourish. To link workings across the River Esk at Gill Force, in December 1880 the South Cumberland Iron Co. even opened a new tramway from Dalegarth Cottages, funded by the Allport family. (A daughter of the late Midland Railway supremo had married a Brocklebank of Irton Hall.) When iron prices slumped, these isolated mines were never profitable again but the passenger services continued.

Five times each day, trains took people to villas in a new village at Eskdale Green, their mail, coal into the valley and granite from a quarry which employed over 50 men. The line advertised a journey into *The English Alps*, but the proprietors were called to explain to Parliament why those *who originally promoted the company were not altogether people who could be trusted.* With mounting opposition to building any further railways in the Lake Counties, the R&ER became both an unwitting influence on the future National Park and a growing attraction in its own right as the *shortest registered railway in Great Britain.*

La'al Rat Trod gained the affectionate nickname amid pleas in the local press for *Preservation*, as it could not be sold to pay off its own creditors or those of the Whitehaven Iron Mines Ltd. which owned half the shares but was now itself in receivership! Often on bank holidays, both locos were steamed to pull packed trains, including the three ordinary coaches strengthened by open goods wagons with benches from Ravenglass Public Hall.

Tourists' attention will be about equally directed between the beauties of nature and the primitive, not to say toylike, railway facilities and furniture. The line became legendary for eccentricities, like a guard who opened every station to sell tickets or would stop anywhere en route for passengers! It was a delightful ride along a winding track in magnificent scenery on *a comic opera collection of relics, yet the primitive simplicity of this extraordinary line seems more in keeping with the peace of the dale and the majesty of the mountains.*

To comply with new laws, airbrakes were fitted in 1895, but they were not used when fly-shunting wagons from a moving passenger train caused the death of Guard Tom Bell at Irton Road on 28 October 1898. Then the only working loco fell on its side at Murthwaite on 10 March 1905. The line was treated lightly until a trespasser wrote to the President of the Board of Trade about the state of the track; Winston Churchill passed James Parkinson's letter to his Railway Inspector who met the Receiver. The railway shut without ceremony on 30 November 1908.

A new Eskdale Railway Co. took over with powers to electrify the route, but it could not pay off old debts let alone rebuild the line. Meanwhile a goods train ran three days a week for the quarry and then Eskdale Mining Co., carrying passengers in the brake van at their own risk! After the mines closed, the Whitehaven News recorded the last train on 30 April 1913, but not a final derailment at Raven Villa. The train crew re-railed the loco in their own time. Mrs Steele was proud that her son Billie confessed at school to playing with the points, but the fine cost her £1!

The locos and coaches lay in their sheds at Ravenglass, wagons rotted in sidings and undergrowth blossomed along the way. Then during the First World War, the *Rat Trod* narrowly escaped the fate of many sidings and one entire railway used at the Western Front. This track was in such bad condition, it was not worth lifting for scrap!

Shortly before closure of the 3ft. gauge, main line wagons are loaded by hand. Devon *stands in the sidings to allow the single coach from the first arrival of the day to be shunted by gravity back into the platform.*

Photo: Mary Fair

8:

La'al Ratty Revived

The Eskdale Railway was unexpectedly reopened in 1915

*'The Smallest Railway in the World' soon after World War 1. The 4-6-2 locomotive **Colossus**, built by Bassett-Lowke, is about to leave Ravenglass from the 3 ft. gauge trainshed. The 4-4-2 locomotive **Sans Pareil** will follow with the second portion in the platform.*
Photo: Mary Fair

DURING the Great War of 1914-18, Ravenglass was a retreat where Sir Edward Elgar and others could forget the conflict, although it lost men as did every corner of the Empire. The Eskdale Railway lay derelict, when three friends came, by the introduction of Aubrey Brocklebank who had a Bassett-Lowke 7¹/4in-gauge garden railway at Irton Hall. The model manufacturer, his partner Robert Mitchell and secretary John Wills walked along the track on a sunny June day and were so impressed that they leased the line for their Narrow Gauge Railways Ltd.

Before the war they had built miniature railways for funfairs and rich men's toys. They hankered to run a proper train service with their tiny quarter-scale model locos, and after an ingenuous note to the Railway Inspectors, a gang began to relay the old rails to a new gauge of only 15in. On its arrival from Norway, the little 4-4-2 *Sans Pareil* started running to Muncaster on 28 August 1915. By the year-end there were daily trains to Murthwaite, and the tracks re-gauged half way to Boot.

They reached Eskdale Green by Easter 1916 and trains *were busier than at any time under the old company!* The small steam locos pulling open coaches were instantly popular in summer, with closed saloons for bad weather and winter. The war brought many shortages yet, apart from major breakdowns, the *Bantam Railway* ran every single day all year round. The local Sanitary Surveyor and Inspector of Nuisances complained to the Board of Trade but the Ratty was serving the community again, carrying the Royal Mail and all the valley's needs and produce on *The Smallest Public Railway in the World*!

In retrospect, it was a miracle the line survived at all, working trains with such tiny engines that passengers were often asked to push them uphill or had time to pick flowers when they ran out of steam. Full-time staff under manager John Wills included the last 3ft. gauge driver, Jack Lister, and young Bert Thompson, a guard who was allowed to drive if there were ladies in the train! There were also enthusiasts who helped Bert Mitchell in summertime for fun as this was the first-ever preserved railway.

Apart from the last months of Boot mine, Beckfoot was the upper terminus until train services were extended to Dalegarth Cottages. On 18 July 1923 the line was *greatly admired by The Queen of Holland,* and in 1927 by the Prince of Wales. Meanwhile, at Ravenglass the old trainshed had its side cladding removed, and tracks spread out around a new bungalow for staff, a carriage shed, turntable and an overhead gantry where broken stone was transferred by tipping wagons.

Throughout the year trains now carried thousands of tons of granite from a quarry at Beckfoot via a new crushing plant 2¹/2 miles away at Murthwaite. Chippings went to local road improvements while railway ballast found a market on the main line. A new 2-8-2 loco was built overscale for freight and reliability, but *River Esk* of 1923 was also model enough for passenger work. *La'al Ratty* was quickly established as a vital part of the district and has supplied its neighbours with a valued commodity.

The gateway to the village is the overbridge carrying La'al Ratty, with Railway Terrace beyond. The original Muir-Hill quarry tractor of 1927 hauls granite wagons past the chute that was used to load roadstone into lorries. Upgrading the main road from Muncaster Mill to Broad Oak was a mainspring of the revival of the R&ER granite traffic from the 1920s.
Photo: Rick Eyles

After a dispute at the Board of Trade, the trackbed was transferred to Sir Aubrey Brocklebank and a fellow ship owner in 1924. For local employment they funded further development, including new stations at each end of the track. In 1926 the line was extended over the mineral trackbed to the present terminus at Dalegarth. A hut from Eskmeals Gun Range was re-erected as a cafe, convenient by the main road for passengers to travel by Sims buses for Wastwater. The winter of 1927 at Ravenglass saw the 3ft trainshed cleared away to allow an open island platform between four parallel tracks, with a new waiting shelter. The old slates went to roof a barn then being converted to a house at Dune View.

However, the daily mail contract ceased, leaving a train for Whitehaven Market on Thursdays only and summertime passenger traffic subordinate to the granite now being moved by i/c locos. There was much new construction and rebuilding of structures, track and rolling stock before the untimely death of Sir Aubrey in 1929. Yet the Little Railway was now strong enough to endure, with new blood on the staff who became as firmly part of the social fabric as the miniature steam locos endeared themselves to visitors.

The number of tourists increased, but the area was isolated and only slowly gained modern services. The last of so many improvements made by Sir Josslyn Pennington

before his death in 1917 was to supply mains water from Muncaster to replace individual wells. While village sewage went into the estuary, the managers of the Church School were reprimanded by the Board of Education for the unauthorised building of water closet toilets! The first telephone had arrived in Ravenglass by 1923, but it was a decade before a public callbox was put by the Reading Room as the village trialled the prototype small Strowger automatic exchange for rural areas. By 1936 a supply from North West Electricity replaced paraffin lamps in homes although street lighting was off and on until 1951.

Only two brand new bungalows were built around the village, while *The Old Thack* itself was demolished in 1923. The shops, bank and blacksmiths were joined by a new garage and the Wilson's taxi service. With the highways much improved after 1925, a new Cumberland Motor Services bus route followed the main road past the War Memorial designed by Sir Edward Lutyens. The historic coach-route along the shore to Eskmeals was still maintained by the District Council, but the Ford across the Mite was *in a very bad state of repair* while the Old Footbridge was *broken down and impassible. Occasionally a coastal tramp boat would beach in the bay on the Eskmeals side of the river to take on a load of gravel.* In spite of thousands of visitors each year to see the new attraction, Ravenglass still held true to its past.

9:

Main Line Through Two Wars

The village became a popular destination for trippers from Blackpool

THE main line saw changes in the First World War. Station lamps were masked after a German submarine shelled the coast near Whitehaven. In 1916 Ravenglass viaduct was strengthened, Furness coaches were outshopped in blue, while Maryport & Carlisle locos ran through on the Mail Train, and London & North Western locos on the *Jellicoe* coal trains.

After the war, the last new locos appeared in FR red, the 4-6-4 tanks built by Kitsons. On 1 January 1923, the Furness Railway became part of the largest regional railway group, the London, Midland & Scottish (LMS). Although Barrow retained District status, some trains now worked from Carlisle to Lancaster and beyond through Ravenglass, the 8.02am M&SO to Euston and the 12.11pm to Preston, while the 8.56pm from Millom terminated here. The Mails arrived each morning dropped from the Down Travelling Post Office into a net just south of Clemlands Creep. The Down goods shunted from 8.45am *to convey Whitehaven cattle on Thursdays and attach Fish traffic.* It was a busy stretch of railway, although ex-Furness engines were soon rarely seen, in favour of standard LMS classes in crimson or black.

At Eskmeals, the branch into the dunes saw considerable extension for Vickers Gun Range and the local granite paving traffic. The hoppers by the Up siding were fed from Waberthwaite Quarry by an overhead cableway, which was used by the manager to make literally flying visits to see production! By comparison, Beckfoot Quarry was isolated. The new R&ER managers wanted to quarry by their crushing plant, but the landowners, Muncaster Estates, did not wish to damage trade at Waberthwaite. But as output from Murthwaite quadrupled, improved productivity inspired a unique branch line as there was just space for standard-gauge open wagons under the roadbridge at Muncaster Mill.

Throughout the summer of 1929, full size sleepers were laid under the 15in gauge metals for 2 miles of interlaced track. At *The Big Points the* small trains ran over *ingenious movable crossings* but looked odd running on the middle rails of what appeared to be double track! In December,

the LMS delivered a Kerr, Stuart 0-6-0 diesel capable of hauling 10 loaded wagons. By April 1932 a Freight Train Meeting at Barrow noted of Trips 61-64: *The traffic from the Ravenglass & Eskdale Railway had increased . . . the shunting and hauling of large quantities of roadstone was affecting the running of the outward trip . . . and very little improvement in the running of the roadside trains could be expected.* By 1934 granite traffic had peaked at 56,000 tons, but this was now supporting the line.

The Divisional Manager even suggested that the LMS should build a mountain railway up Scafell, as Eskdale was now attracting such crowds on the weekly excursions from Morecambe and Blackpool via Furness Abbey, Keswick and Shap. When the *Lakes Restaurant Car* specials arrived, passengers queued across Ravenglass yard for tickets. One train would go with *River Irt*, the second hauled by *Esk,* and the third a collection of covered coaches hauled by *River Mite.* Worked on time interval between the quarry trains, the R&ER became a busy operation in summer time with over 50 staff.

As stone traffic slumped in 1937 negotiations took place with the Keswick Granite Company (newly formed from the Cumberland Granite Quarry, Embleton and Threlkeld Granite), which had closed its 2ft 4in gauge line along St Johns-in-the-Vale. The Eskdale line was valued at £ 22,000 but did not change hands, though it lost the Thursdays only service for Whitehaven market. With the outbreak of the Second World War, the little railway closed to passengers but the output of ballast continued.

The Beacon on Newtown Knott was demolished to remove a landmark as Hitler's panzers swept over Europe. In May 1940, 50 sheep crossed the Ratty fences to damage a hayfield near Rock Point, and start a long Court case. Although there were munitions factories close by to north and south, with treasured artwork from the Tate Gallery evacuated to Muncaster Castle, this coast was largely ignored by enemy aircraft, apart from a land mine which exploded on the shore rocking Ravenglass station area. Stationmaster Harry Parker had a much reduced service, with no passenger trains from 12.18pm to 4.16pm.

*On the busiest day ever thus far, 20 August 1933, R&ER rebuilt 0-8-2 **River Irt** arrives in the narrow-gauge railway's station. No less than four hundred and ninety-one passengers crowd onto the Down main platform at Ravenglass to continue on to Keswick by the Lakes Restaurant Car special from Blackpool.*
Photo: Mary Fair

Ex-LMS Class 5 4-6-0 No.44758 crosses the four-span viaduct over the River Mite. Stanier-designed locomotives dominated services from the 1930s to the last excursion before the end of local BR steam, **The Northman** *on 10 October 1967. A new resort was planned to be built beside the track here in the 1880s. Photo: Douglas Ferreira*

In May 1945 R&ER passenger services were quickly resumed, and peace was duly celebrated with a trip on Ratty, sports on the Green and tea in the Public Hall on 13 July. Traditions continued with manager Harry Hilton arriving as Santa with presents for village children. *River Irt* was back in steam by 1947 but, unlike the main line, its route was excluded from the Nationalisation of Britain's railways on 1 January 1948. In 1949 however the Keswick Granite Co. finally secured its purchase, reeling with orders to supply the insatiable demand for aggregate to build the nuclear installations on the site of Windscale Ordnance factory at Sellafield.

As the village starred in two BBC broadcasts, the Little Railway was well supported, and saw *River Esk* returned to service in 1952. For Coronation Year, the waiting shelters were suitably decorated by Florrie Hilton, who had produced a Muncaster Pageant two years before at the Castle. The people of the district told the story of their community but were amazed when it attracted an audience of 10,000! Alas, the Flower Show which continued the traditions of the ancient fair had faltered in 1951.

While the R&ER made steady losses for its new owners, Beckfoot quarry had closed in 1953, its stone uneconomic to produce. The standard gauge track from Murthwaite was quickly removed and the diesel loco taken off by road, surviving in work to be preserved at length on the Foxfield Railway. The parent Keswick Granite Co. had tried to sell the Eskdale Railway but its legal title through South Cumberland Granite Co. was confused, the moribund earlier companies a factor which put off any interested party. In desperation during 1960, the undertaking was to be disposed by *Auction as one lot or 60* on 10 August and its future was in the balance once more.

On 14 July 1960, Muncaster Parish Council made some historic decisions for Ravenglass. It stated the port was open for boating or fishing without licence. Claims based on the Agreement of King John in 1208 that *the village green belongs to the Lord of the Manor* were countered. It opposed conversion of the Public Hall to flats, and leased the building under a registered charity. A fundamental step in saving a unique part of the newly designated Lake District National Park, La'al Ratty itself, was the catalyst turning public reaction into action to Save the Little Railway.

The LMS Up Roadside Goods on 5 December 1929 delivers a brand-new standard gauge 0-6-0 diesel locomotive built by Kerr, Stuart of Stoke-on-Trent for service on the dual-gauge interlaced section of the R&ER to Murthwaite Crushing Plant. Photo: Mary Fair

10:

Save our Railways

Threatened with closure, both local rail links prevail against the odds.

OPPOSING almost certain closure, the Revd Murray Hodges swung the Councillors to support moves to save La'al Ratty. The Parish Council and its Clerk, Douglas Robinson, became the trustee for funds raised by the *Ravenglass & Eskdale Railway Preservation Society*, newly formed by a group of Barrow railwaymen. The public appeal was now backed by Colin Gilbert, a Society life member who had drawn back earlier from buying the line himself, and by Sir Wavell Wakefield MP.

At the Auction at Gosforth on 7 September 1960, the Society's bid of £12,000 was accepted. Its fundamental role and its contribution of £5,000 was then recognised in equity within the new Company, formed by its trustees to operate the line. With growing traffic, and the enduring financial and practical support of those founding trustees, Colin Gilbert, the Wakefield family and the Preservation Society, the R&ER has seen the longest period of security since its first inception.

From that point in 1961 an ongoing process began of complete renewal of the line and passenger stock. Where grass grew over rotting track, full-time staff and volunteers have laid new rails and hardwood sleepers throughout. At Ravenglass the tracks in the station have altered with new platforms and traditional signals; however the innovative use of radio signalling introduced after the line's centenary means its route appears little changed but is safely operated. The original 1875 loco shed and Irton Road Station survive intact from 3ft gauge times.

There are few days when a hoot is not heard. Among the fleet, 5 steam locos do much of the work in the daily running season, extended from 5 to 9 months of the year. Diesels work early trains, some days carrying school children. Trains have unique open coaches in good weather and heated saloons in winter, giving a ride through ever-changing scenery enjoyed annually by over 150,000 passengers and many supporting helpers.

No sooner was La'al Ratty secured than its neighbour faced a total loss of passenger services. In the Beeching Plan for British Railways (BR), all stations from Barrow to Whitehaven were to close. In the event the small stations lost their staff and their goods yard facilities. Ravenglass signalbox was closed and the points locked out of use on 9 February 1965. With retirement of Stationmaster/ Porter Tommy Brocklebank, the Pullman Camping Coaches only recently arrived departed for Seascale.

Freight hauled by a variety of ex-LMS and BR Standard steam locos used the capacity of the single lines beyond Sellafield. Two southbound iron ore trains daily from Beckermet to Millom coloured the Up line deep red quickly after reballasting. Passenger trains were worked by the Metro-Vic 'Type B' Co-Bos based at Barrow. Regular excursions included the *John Peel Land Cruise* using Derby Lightweight Diesel Multiple Units from Morecambe to Keswick via Workington. Introduced south of Whitehaven a decade after pioneer services north to Carlisle, the danger from their quiet running led to completion of a footbridge along the viaduct across the Mite in 1964.

When Workington shed closed to steam in December 1967, freight was worked by Clayton 'Type 1' Bo-Bos. D8505 made the final rail movement into Ravenglass with the return on 20 September 1968 of the Camping Coaches *Elmira* and *Maid of Kent,* after which the last standard-gauge siding and loop was lifted the following week by Thomas Wards of Sheffield. One incident was the derailment of the Whitehaven-bound Marchon oil tank train on 21 November 1969. Thankfully, thousands of gallons of thick oil spilled near the Roman fort were kept from polluting the estuary. A collapsed underbridge was redecked in concrete. British Rail passengers now used Class 108 DMUs, except for coaches attached to the Sunday evening Whitehaven-Huddersfield Travelling Post Office until October 1974. After other stations became Request Stops in 1977, *Ravenglass for Eskdale* regained its old status.

The last chance for many to travel on La'al Ratty just prior to the Auction. On 4 September 1960, the Stephenson Locomotive Society had a special train from Leeds, returning via Keswick, and here hauled by ex-LMS 'Patriot' Class 4-6-0 No.45503 The Royal Leicestershire Regiment. Photo: John Hammond

Much of the BR station was sold to the Ravenglass & Eskdale Railway to secure the goods yard for its car park, and the former Up loop for the proposed Muncaster Castle Extension Railway which was not progressed although approval was granted in 1971. The cattle dock had been removed earlier, providing stone edging for the halts at Muncaster Mill and Beckfoot. The awning over R&ER Platform 3 follows the original company boundary. This awning was rescued from Millom Down Platform to join the Furness Railway footbridge from Coniston and some 'Squirrel' seats. With the Platform 1 awning using FR columns from Whitehaven Bransty, the station gained a Railway Heritage award.

The Furness Railway main building was converted into the *Ratty Arms* pub, opened on 13 June 1974. The goods shed was a woodwork and paintshop until 1981, then a factory for Clupet Piston Rings before becoming the main engineering workshop, rebuilding locos for Blackpool Pleasure Beach and making new steam locos for Shuzen-ji in Japan. The Up platform building became Ravenglass Railway Museum in 1978, and a small shelter served travellers to Barrow thereafter.

The years from 1973 saw special steam excursion trains, with regular operations of *The Cumbrian Coast Express*. Most preserved main line steam locos have called at

Ravenglass and departed south to whistles from La'al Ratty alongside. Steam hauled the *150th Anniversary Travelling Post Office* on the Up line before withdrawal on 27 September 1991. The extensive line through Eskmeals Proof & Experimental ranges was closed and lifted in 1994 just before its centenary, and is remembered by the plate of its last loco, Army No. 431 *Muncaster Castle*.

When Muncaster Estates owned much of the village, change was restricted but society was stimulated by a throughput of people working at Sellafield. Then on 27 February 1967, spring tides, strong winds and high rivers combined to flood the village. Where the green sloped down to the beach this was declared as common land and built up obscuring the foundations etc. of *Gibraltar Row*. Overnight, on 11 November 1978, waves broke through to flood the west side of Main Street, with a boat driven into the back of the new Post Office. Water forced up drains soiled homes, and this was to change Ravenglass radically.

To protect the village, seawalls closed off the old cart lanes to the beach, with massive steel gates at Town End across the ancient coachroad to Crosswater, and berms along the village green, all useless without a sealed sewer along the shore to a treatment plant with the capacity not only for the existing village but also for developments. A caravan site, public toilets, and housing estate quickly followed. Croftlands Drive and

A pair of immaculate BR English Electric Type 4 1-Co-Co-1s work the Presidential Train returning HE Ayub Khan of Pakistan from a visit to the nuclear installations at Sellafield in November 1966. The cattle dock and goods shed siding have gone, but the camping coaches Elmira *and* Maid of Kent *await their final return journey to Seascale before the last tracks were lifted.*
Photo: Douglas Ferreira

Townfield Close echoed ancient names while Murrayfield Terrace recognised the Vicar who had done so much for this Parish. Construction was monitored by the Lake District Special Planning Board, concerned by the loss of Muncaster School in 1981 and other threats to the community. A Conservation Area designated key structures, declaring the village had unique value. It also protected the original R&ER loco shed and agricultural buildings.

While The Barns became housing, Holman's workshop and Pharoah's Garage vanished with barely a trace. Fenwick's Butchers, which made a mile of Cumberland sausage one week in 1977, became a craft shop. Freed from block ownership, the village lost grey rendered walls and dark blue paintwork for pastels. However, local people united against National River Authority proposals to create an outer barrier or reinforce the back walls of the seaside properties. The risk of the worst floods in 50 years was preferred to the loss of the organic sense that the village grew out of the sands.

Ravenglass rarely makes a mark on the outside world, although in 1983 a bin of silt from the estuary blocked London's traffic through Whitehall. After completion of the THORP plant, the village had fewer workers at Sellafield and lacked winter trade to keep the Pennington Arms Hotel

open after September 1996. Yet it had enough vitality to restart the Charter Fair in the spirit of 1209, raising funds for local causes including the Parish Hall, Waberthwaite School, and the restoration of St Michael's Church, reopened on 14 March 1999.

The site of the Roman Fort was cleared of trees in recognition of its protected status; the bonfires recalled the strife within this ancient place. The R&ER was given the *Ian Allan National Railway Heritage Award* for restoration of the Furness Railway signal box, an auspicious launch to the *Ratty 125* celebrations. The new century saw Muncaster Castle restore its buildings and garden, while Ravenglass expressed a strong community spirit with thriving groups from Boating Association to Village Forum.

150 years after steam train replaced stagecoach and horses, rail and restored bus links ran every day. Railcars built in Workington by Leyland Bus worked passenger services from 1990; BR Class 153 single unit Sprinters and 142 Pacers were franchised on 2 March 1997, initially branded *North Western Trains*, then *First North Western*. Freights hauled by red *English, Welsh & Scottish* Class 37 and 66 locos run amongst the frequent movements for British Nuclear Fuels at Sellafield behind by their Class 20 and 37 machines in *Direct Rail Services* dark blue.

The worst floods in living memory occurred on 27 February 1967, although the Market Cross and the Poor House behind had been deluged oft times before. Repeated on 11 November 1978, further flooding of Main Street has since been prevented by the building of sea walls and the storm gate.
Photo: Cliff Turner

*2-8-2 locomotive **River Esk** awaits departure in 1979 from R&ER Platform 3 under the ex-Millom Down platform awning.*
Photo: Nick Stanbra

Historians class Ravenglass as *a failed town* which fell in the railway revolution. But had George Stephenson built his high speed West Coast route to Scotland there would certainly be no station here, let alone one refurbished for the 21st Century! This unique coastal village of the Lake District National Park can be reached by the most delightful rail journeys.

We do not know of any other place, on which so many praises and abuses have been lavished ... Ravenglass is either better than Paradise or worse than Purgatory ... to all who wish to settle the question of the scenic or social merits of Ravenglass, we shall merely say - Go and judge for yourselves!
(Handbook of the Whitehaven & Furness Junction Railway 1851)

Ravenglass Railway Station

The up-line platform bridges a metal road
That slopes unwalled to salt and sand, and boats
Anchored in green-webbed goosefoot and sea aster,
Tarred spars and bendwaters, the cockly trod
Of stumps that mark the ebb-track of the ford.
Here where a blathering, Ulster storm
Chivies in autumn the tide through the bar of the dunes,
Annexing tar and tarmac for the Irish Sea,
Children, waiting for a train, and nosing
End to end of a station long as a Blackpool pier
Can drop their pennies between the wooden planks
Full splash into the water. The storm
Rolls up and over like a drum, leaving
The little auk and the fork-tailed petrel
Brained against telegraph poles; shore-side chimneys
Breathe heavy as horses into the mist; each tree,
Backjacked to the wind, arms high from the shoulder,
Twists in a tatter and tangle of brown
Like a boy pulling his jersey over his head.
Here camped the Romans, sweating in thermal saloons,
Bragging their autobiographies like dice
(A raped virgin beats a burnt town) -

Then in the exilic not-quite-dark, they peedled
Down past the boundary ditch to the huts and the girls,
Warm beds and Welsh voices, while yonder
The dunes, as now, drifted in the purple rain.
Here, too, in the winter of war, the children came,
A Tyneside tang smoking from the stretched larynx,
And here the gold and graphite of the Tate,
Crated and stacked like lemons.
The wagons twitch their toes, the engine blows its nose,
Wheels, rods and pistons bulge and blur in the spray,
And eighty tons of steel float easily away,
Light as suds in the breath of a child. But here
In the fog-sodden fields, under the rain-eaten
Dish-clout of the dykes, among the wrack and rubble
Of the gull-rummaged estuary, or hidden behind
The one-eyed wink of the ticket-seller's window - here
Is the root of a race, clamped tight to the rock,
Wringing from the earth its last few drops of green
Long years after the once-tall trunk is down.

Norman Nicholson

(by permission of Faber & Faber)